# GAME BREAKERS

by James Gigliotti

## SCHOLASTIC INC.

New York     Toronto     London     Auckland
Sydney    Mexico City    New Delhi    Hong Kong

# GAME BREAKERS

**NFL**

All photos © **Getty Images**.

**Front cover (left to right):** Gene Lower; Joe Robbins; Matthew Stockman

**Back Cover (left to right):** Scott Boehm; David Drapkin; Andy Lyons

**Interior:** Title page, left to right (top row): Scott Boehm; Scott Cunningham; Andy Lyons; (bottom row): Paul Jasienski; Tom Dahlin; (3) Evan Pinkus; (4) Chris Trotman; (5 )Matthew Stockman; (6, 15, 22) Scott Boehm; (7, 16, 23) Kevin Terrell; (8) Jeff Gross; (9) Josh Umphrey; (10) Jim Rogash; (11) Chris McGrath; (12) Hunter Martin; (13) Jim McIssac; (14) Rob Tringali; (17) David Drapkin; (18) G. Newman Lowrance; (19, 27) Ronald Martinez; (20, 30) George Gojkovich; (21) Christian Petersen; (24) Paul Spinelli; (25) Scott Cunningham; (26) A. Messerschmidt; (28) Wesley Hitt; (29) Joe Robbins; (31) Win McNamee; (32) Al Pereira

ISBN-13: 978-0-545-13124-7
ISBN-10: 0-545-13124-3

Published by Scholastic Inc.
SCHOLASTIC and associated logos are trademarks and/or registered trademarks of Scholastic Inc.

12 11 10 9 8 7 6 5 4 3 2 1          9 10 11 12 13 14/0

Designed by Cheung Tai
Printed in the U.S.A.
First Scholastic printing, July 2009

ELI MANNING

# ELI MANNING
## QB, GIANTS

For a long time, Eli Manning was known simply as Peyton Manning's little brother — the guy Peyton picked on in some funny television commercials. Sure, Eli was a pretty good quarterback himself in college at Mississippi. He was the top pick of the 2004 NFL Draft, and he had a couple of excellent seasons with the New York Giants. It was Peyton, though, who had all the Pro Bowl seasons with the Indianapolis Colts, plus a Super Bowl championship ring.

Then everything changed in the span of just a few plays in Super Bowl XLII in the 2007 season. Eli and the underdog Giants trailed the powerful New England Patriots 14–10 with time running out in the fourth quarter. It looked as if New York's upset bid was over when Eli was swarmed by several Patriots' pass rushers. But somehow Eli escaped from the pile. He threw a long pass downfield. Wide receiver David Tyree made an acrobatic catch.

Moments later, Eli found wide receiver Plaxico Burress wide open in the end zone. Touchdown! The Giants won 17–14. Eli was named the Most Valuable Player of New York's dramatic Super Bowl victory. He wasn't just Peyton's kid brother anymore. Now fans all over the country knew him as a Super Bowl winner, too.

Fueled by the confidence he gained in the 2007 postseason, Eli had his best overall year in 2008. He passed for more than 3,000 yards (3,238) and more than 20 touchdowns (21) for the fourth year in a row. He cut his interceptions in half (from 20 in 2007 to only 10 in 2008). His passer rating was 86.4, his highest ever.

For the first time in his five-season career, Eli made the Pro Bowl. Naturally, Peyton was there, too (for the ninth time). It was the first time that two brothers ever played quarterback in the NFL's annual all-star game in the same season.

DREW BREES

# DREW BREES
## QB, SAINTS

A shoulder injury might be devastating to an NFL quarterback's career. For Drew Brees, though, it turned out to be a blessing in disguise. "It's probably the best thing that ever happened to me because it brought me to New Orleans," he said.

The injury occurred in the final game of the 2005 season, when Drew was playing for the San Diego Chargers. He was in his fourth season as the Chargers' starting quarterback. Drew had some good years for San Diego, including a Pro Bowl season in 2004. But the Chargers had a young quarterback named Philip Rivers who was ready to take over. After Brees got injured, San Diego decided not to sign him to a new contract.

Drew's shoulder injury scared off a lot of other teams, too. Not the Saints, though. They had some promising young players on offense and needed a proven quarterback who could get the ball to them.

Drew got the ball to them so much in his first season in New Orleans that he set a club record by passing for 4,418 yards in 2006. The next year, he broke his own mark by passing for 4,423 yards. But he was just getting warmed up. In 2008, Drew had one of the most prolific passing seasons in NFL history. He became only the second man ever to pass for more than 5,000 yards in a season. His 5,069 yards through the air were only 15 yards short of Dan Marino's record 5,084 yards for the Miami Dolphins in 1984. Drew's 34 touchdown passes tied for the league lead (with Rivers) and set another club record.

Drew made the Pro Bowl in 2008 for the second time in his three seasons in New Orleans. He earned NFL Offensive Player of the Years honors from the Associated Press.

Turns out that shoulder injury was the best thing that ever happened to the Saints, too.

PHILIP RIVERS

# PHILIP RIVERS
## QB, CHARGERS

When Philip Rivers first took over as San Diego's starting quarterback in 2006, his primary job was clear: hand off the ball to LaDainian Tomlinson and let the Chargers' superstar running back do his thing. "LT" almost single-handedly carried San Diego to back-to-back playoff appearances in Rivers' first two years as a starter.

By late in the 2008 season, though, things had changed. Tomlinson was hurting, and the Chargers were struggling. At 4–8, San Diego looked as if it wouldn't make the playoffs. But that's when Philip took over.

First, the former North Carolina State star passed for three touchdowns in San Diego's rout of the Oakland Raiders. Then he rallied his team from 18 points behind to beat the Kansas City Chiefs. He passed for the winning touchdown late in the fourth quarter.

The next week, Philip passed for a career-best of four touchdowns in a victory at Tampa Bay. And finally, he was almost perfect in a season-ending showdown against Denver for the AFC West championship. He completed 15 of 20 passes for 207 yards and two touchdowns, with no interceptions, as San Diego won 52–21. Remarkably, the Chargers were in the playoffs once again. "We obviously went a different route than we thought we would," Rivers said after the division-clinching victory. "But we're here." Once in the postseason, San Diego upset the Indianapolis Colts. Only a loss to eventual Super Bowl–champion Pittsburgh ended the Chargers' title hopes.

For the season, Philip passed for a career-best 4,009 yards and a club-record 34 touchdowns. He led the NFL with a passer rating of 105.5, another San Diego record. Those are impressive feats for a franchise that includes the great Dan Fouts among its all-time quarterbacks.

The most impressive feat of all, though? By the end of the 2008 season, the Chargers were no longer considered LaDainian Tomlinson's team. Philip had become San Diego's new team leader.

CHAD PENNINGTON

# CHAD PENNINGTON
## QB, DOLPHINS

**L**ess than a month before the start of the 2008 season, Chad Pennington didn't have a job.

Pennington had been the starting quarterback for the New York Jets for much of the previous eight years. But when the Jets traded for veteran Brett Favre during the preseason, they let Chad go.

It was a tough way for Pennington to end his time in New York. He had started 61 of the 70 games that he played for the Jets since being drafted out of Marshall University in the first round in 2000. One thing Jets fans learned over the years, though, was never to count Chad out.

For instance, it looked like Chad's career was in jeopardy when he had two shoulder surgeries in 2005. Instead, he was back in the lineup in 2006, leading the Jets to the playoffs and earning the NFL's Comeback Player of the Year Award.

After the Jets let Chad go, he signed with the Miami Dolphins, one of New York's big rivals in the AFC's Eastern Division. The Dolphins had gone a disastrous 1-15 the season before.

It took Chad only two weeks to earn Miami's starting job. Then he passed for a career-best 3,653 yards and 19 touchdowns during the 2008 regular season. His completion percentage of 67.4 was the highest mark in the league that year. Once again, he was named the NFL's Comeback Player of the Year. "That award says an awful lot about Chad and all the hard work he's put in," Miami coach Tony Sparano said.

More importantly, the Dolphins equaled the greatest one-season turnaround in NFL history. The club that won only one game in 2007 won 11 games and made the playoffs in Chad's first year in Miami.

On the final day of the 2008 regular season, Chad passed for 200 yards and 2 touchdowns to lead the Dolphins to a 24-17 victory that put them in the playoffs. That win, coincidentally, came against the Jets in New York.

Jets fans thus were reminded what Dolphins fans knew now, too: Never count Chad out.

BRIAN WESTBROOK

# BRIAN WESTBROOK
## RB, EAGLES

Brian Westbrook is the man who makes the Eagles' offense go. He runs the ball. He catches the ball. He scores more touchdowns than anyone else on the team. All of that keeps opposing defensive coordinators awake at night before their team plays Philadelphia! They've got to find a way to stop the Eagles' superstar running back.

Not many teams have. Although slowed by injuries much of the 2008 season, Brian still managed to gain 1,338 yards from scrimmage (rushing and receiving). That gave him 9,930 yards in only 99 games in his career — an excellent average of a little more than 100 yards per game.

Brian remained effective despite knees that hurt so badly late in the 2008 season that he couldn't even practice with the team a lot of times. He'd study the Eagles' game plan. He'd watch lots of video of the team the Eagles were playing that week. Then, on Sunday he'd go out and score a touchdown! In all, Brian reached the end zone 14 times in 2008 — nine times on runs and five times catching passes. That was the most in one season in his seven-year career.

Brian originally joined the Eagles as a third-round draft pick out of Villanova in 2002. In his early seasons with the team, he proved his worth as a pass catcher. Over the years, though, he has run the ball from scrimmage more and more. In 2007, he gained a career-best 1,333 yards on the ground. He also caught 90 passes that year. It was one of the highest totals by a running back in NFL history. His 2,104 yards from scrimmage led the league — which is why other coaches have to worry so much about stopping him.

"I would give him the ball almost every down," said Adrian Peterson, the Vikings' superstar running back. The Eagles don't do that. It only seems that way.

THOMAS JONES

# THOMAS JONES
## RB, JETS

**T**homas Jones took the long way to the Pro Bowl in Honolulu, Hawaii, in the 2008 season. For one thing, Honolulu is more than 5,000 miles from his hometown of Big Stone Gap, Virginia. For another, he made stops in Arizona, Tampa Bay, and Chicago before making the NFL's annual all-star game for the first time while playing for the New York Jets.

Thomas also didn't get to the Pro Bowl until he was 30 years old. That's a ripe old age for NFL running backs. Their bodies take a lot of pounding from all the times they are slammed to the ground by opposing tacklers. At an age when most running backs start to decline, though, Thomas had his best year yet. He ran for 1,312 yards. He gained 1,519 yards from scrimmage (that's rushing plus receiving), which was the most of his nine-year career. Most importantly, he scored 15 touchdowns. That was another career best, and it equaled the third-highest total in the NFL in 2008. It also was a big step up from the two touchdowns that he scored in 2007.

Thomas' teammates recognized his value to the Jets. Not only did they vote him as the team's most valuable player for 2008, but they voted for him as their most inspirational player, too.

Thomas' big season was a far cry from the early days of his career. For a long time, in fact, NFL teams had a hard time trying to figure out exactly what they had in Jones. They all agreed that he had talent. The Arizona Cardinals even made him the seventh player picked in the 2000 draft. But Thomas bounced around from city to city for several years. Every team for which he played felt they had someone else who could do the job better. That is, until the Jets traded for him before the 2007 season. Now the only place he's going is up.

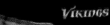

ADRIAN PETERSON

# ADRIAN PETERSON
## RB, VIKINGS

**R**unning back Adrian Peterson's nickname is "All Day." As in, he can run the ball all day long. As in, defenses have to work all day long to stop him. As in . . . well, you get the idea.

Some people call the Minnesota Vikings superstar "AD" for short. Other folks call him "AP" for his initials. Maybe they should just call him "NFL rushing champion," because that's what Adrian was in only his second season in the league in 2008. That year, his 1,760 yards on the ground marked the most in a season in Vikings' history.

Big, strong, and fast, Adrian can make opposing tacklers miss with his shifty moves — or he can run right over them with his awesome power. "He's as physical a man as I've ever seen play running back," former Tampa Bay head coach Jon Gruden once said about him.

There may be no bigger game breaker in the league today than Adrian. In 2008, 42 of his 363 carries went for 10 or more yards. He had three long gains of 50 or more yards.

All of that proved that Adrian's rookie season in 2007 was no fluke. A first-round draft pick out of Oklahoma (he was the seventh overall choice), Adrian ran for 1,341 yards — the most ever by a Vikings' rookie. In his very first game, he showed how good he can be. He took a short pass from quarterback Tarvaris Jackson and burst upfield for a 60-yard touchdown. Several weeks later, Adrian had the best single-game rushing mark in NFL history: 296 yards in a victory over San Diego.

Adrian needed only 21 NFL games to reach 2,000 yards rushing in his career. Only two players in league history ever reached that mark any faster, and they're both among the all-time greats: Eric Dickerson (who needed 18 games) and Earl Campbell (20 games).

By whatever name you call him, Adrian already is an NFL superstar.

WES WELKER

# WES WELKER
## WR, PATRIOTS

It would be hard to pick out Wes Welker as a football player in a crowd. At 5-feet-9 inches and 185 pounds, he could just as easily be an insurance agent or a financial analyst than an NFL star. And when he stands next to fellow Patriots' pass catchers such as 6-feet-4 inch, 215-pound wide receiver Randy Moss or 6-feet-3 inch, 255-pound tight end Benjamin Watson, he hardly looks as if he fits in.

As the old saying goes, though, good things come in small packages. While Moss and other players in New England grab most of the headlines, it was Welker who made the Pro Bowl in the 2008 season. That year he caught 111 passes. His total was the second most in the NFL that season, behind only the 115 receptions by Houston's Andre Johnson. It was the second most in Patriots' history, behind only the 112 catches Wes had in 2007. In fact, he became only the eighth player in NFL history to catch more than 100 passes in back-to-back seasons.

Want more numbers? His 223 receptions over the 2007 and 2008 seasons were the most in the NFL in that span. In 2008, he had at least six catches in each of the Patriots' first 11 games. That was the longest such streak to start a season in league history.

Wes came to the Patriots in trade with the Miami Dolphins in 2007. Although he had a stellar college career, he was not drafted out of Texas Tech, mostly because of his size. He played briefly for San Diego in 2004 before moving on to Miami, which used him mainly as a kick returner.

New England head coach Bill Belichick, though, recognized that Wes had other talents, too. "We played against him twice a year, and we couldn't handle him," says Belichick.

Wes may be little, but he has become a big part of the Patriots' offense.

ANDRE JOHNSON

# ANDRE JOHNSON
## WR, TEXANS

n 2006, the first time that Gary Kubiak met star wide receiver Andre Johnson, the new Houston Texans' head coach had a message for him. "I'd like you to catch one hundred balls," Kubiak told him.

That was music to Andre's ears. Every wide receiver wants to catch 100 passes. That's a magical number for them. It's like a baseball player hitting 50 home runs in a season or a basketball player averaging 30 points per game for a whole year. Ordinary players don't reach those totals. It takes a star to get there. And Kubiak knew he had a star pass catcher in Johnson.

Andre, who was in his fourth NFL season at the time, proved his coach's faith in him by catching a club-record 103 passes in 2006. He was hurt for much of 2007, and then had the best year of his career in 2008. He led the NFL that season by catching 115 passes. His 1,575 receiving yards also was the best in the league. He was an easy choice to make the Pro Bowl for the third time.

Andre, who played college football at Miami, was the third overall pick of the 2003 draft. He has all the tools NFL coaches and scouts look for in a great wide receiver. He is fast enough to work the outside of the field and catch long passes. At 6-feet-3 inches and 219 pounds, he's also big enough and tough enough to work inside. On top of all that, he is a tireless worker who is always trying to get better. In fact, Kubiak calls Andre "as hard a worker as I've ever been around." That's high praise considering that Kubiak once was an assistant coach for a San Francisco 49ers' team that included Jerry Rice. That all-time great wide receiver's work ethic was legendary.

With all those things going for him, there's no telling how good Andre can be.

CALVIN JOHNSON

# CALVIN JOHNSON
## WR, LIONS

t's hard to find many good things to say about a year with no wins and 16 losses. But for Lions' fans, the one bright spot in a disastrous season in 2008 was the play of Calvin Johnson. That year, Johnson emerged as one of the top wide receivers in the NFL.

Calvin joined the Lions as the second overall pick of the 2007 draft. In his final season at Georgia Tech in 2006, he won the Biletnikoff Award as college football's best receiver. Right away, he showed flashes of potential as a rookie with the Lions. He caught a touchdown pass in his very first game. He caught another in his second. By season's end, he had 48 catches, including four for touchdowns, and 756 receiving yards.

That was a pretty good start. But it was nothing compared to what Calvin did in 2008. He caught 78 passes that season for 1,331 yards. His 12 touchdown catches tied for the NFL lead with the Arizona Cardinals' Larry Fitzgerald. Calvin had at least 100 receiving yards in a game five times. He caught at least one touchdown pass in 10 of Detroit's 16 games. One of his scoring catches covered 96 yards. He also had big-play touchdown receptions of 70, 47, 38, and 33 yards.

Calvin did all that even though the Lions didn't have a lot of other good players on offense. That meant defenses could concentrate on stopping him without bothering too much about the other guys. Still, they discovered that he was tough to stop.

Only the Lions' dismal record kept Calvin from making the Pro Bowl. "He might not have been selected to the Pro Bowl," said Rod Marinelli, who was Detroit's coach in 2008, "but he has gotten the attention of coaches all over this league."

For Calvin, his big season in 2008 didn't mean a lot because it didn't help his team win. But with a new coach and new players around their star wide receiver, the Lions have plenty of hope for 2009 . . . and beyond!

LARRY FITZGERALD

# LARRY FITZGERALD
## WR, CARDINALS

In the 2008 postseason, fans all across the country discovered what Arizona's opponents have known for a long time: Larry Fitzgerald is one of the NFL's best players.

The sure-handed wide receiver has been productive ever since the Cardinals selected him out of Pittsburgh with the third overall pick in the 2004 draft. He caught a whopping 330 passes and made the Pro Bowl twice in his first four seasons in the desert. Still, he was relatively anonymous while playing for a team that had not won a championship of any kind in more than 60 years.

In 2008, though, Arizona won the NFC Western Division championship for first time. Larry caught 96 passes, including 12 for touchdowns. The team limped into the postseason, though, with four losses in its last six regular-season games. Then the Cardinals caught fire in the playoffs. Larry was a big reason why. He set NFL records by catching 30 passes for 546 yards and seven touchdowns in four postseason games, including the Super Bowl.

Time and again in the 2008 postseason, Larry proved he has two of the best hands in the game. No matter where the pass was thrown, he plucked the ball out of the air, often in spectacular fashion. "He's the best at going up and coming down with the ball," says the Texans' Andre Johnson, a star wide receiver himself.

Against the Pittsburgh Steelers in Super Bowl XLIII, Larry was quiet until the fourth quarter. Then he helped Arizona pull off a stunning rally. First, he leaped high in the end zone to catch a touchdown pass from Kurt Warner. Later in the period, he took a short pass from Warner and scooted 64 yards right through the middle of the Steelers' defense for a go-ahead touchdown.

The Cardinals eventually lost the game in the final seconds. Still, Larry wasn't done. The next week, he was in Honolulu for the Pro Bowl. He caught a pair of touchdown passes in the NFC's 30-21 victory and was named the Player of the Game.

DALLAS CLARK

# DALLAS CLARK
## TE, COLTS

Game-breaking tight ends have been all the rage in the NFL for several seasons. From San Diego's Antonio Gates to Kansas City's Tony Gonzalez to Dallas' Jason Witten, these players give their quarterbacks a big target in the passing game.

A tight end who combines such receiving skills with the more-traditional blocking responsibility of a tight end is extra valuable. And perhaps no tight end in the league combines them as well as Dallas Clark of the Indianapolis Colts.

In 2008, Dallas set a franchise record for tight ends (breaking his own record) by catching 77 passes. He also set another team mark for a tight end with 848 receiving yards. That broke a record held by John Mackey, who is in the Pro Football Hall of Fame.

Many of Dallas' receptions come in traffic over the middle, in front of defensive backs and linebackers in pass coverage. That means Dallas knows he's going to get crunched by defenders almost every time he catches the ball. "It's an ugly part of the job," he says. But he also figures that if he's going to get hit anyway, he might as well hold onto the ball!

In addition to his pass-catching ability, Dallas also plays a big part in the Colts' rushing attack. At 6-feet-3 inches and 257 pounds, he's like an extra offensive lineman on running plays. He also sometimes provides extra pass protection for Peyton Manning when the Colts' quarterback gets the ball downfield to star wide receivers Reggie Wayne, Marvin Harrison, and Anthony Gonzalez.

That kind of versatility sets Dallas apart from a lot of other good receiving tight ends. Surprisingly, though, he hasn't made the Pro Bowl — yet. The Pro Bowl tight ends usually get there mostly for their receiving skills. But even if Dallas hasn't been named an all-star, his teammates know how important he is. "We would not be the same offense without him," Manning says.

# DEMARCUS WARE
## LB, COWBOYS

**E**arly in the opening period of the Dallas Cowboys' Week 16 game against Baltimore in 2008, the Ravens had the ball deep in their own territory. Dallas linebacker DeMarcus Ware burst past Baltimore tackle Adam Terry. Ware was so fast at the snap of the ball that Terry couldn't even get a hand on him. DeMarcus got to quarterback Joe Flacco. He forced a fumble that the Cowboys recovered at the 4-yard line. They scored a touchdown three plays later.

DeMarcus' big play marked his 20th sack of the season. That total put the Cowboys' star in some pretty select company. He became only the seventh player since the NFL made sacks an official statistic in 1982 to get 20 sacks in one season.

Those are the kinds of game-breaking plays that the Cowboys expected when they drafted DeMarcus with the 11th overall pick in 2005. Ware, who is 6-feet-4 inches and 247 pounds, was a star defensive end in college at Troy in a 4-3 alignment. That means a team has four down linemen (DeMarcus was one of them) and three linebackers. The Cowboys wanted DeMarcus to be a linebacker in a 3-4 alignment. That means three down linemen and four linebackers.

DeMarcus made the switch without any trouble. He had eight sacks as a rookie in 2005. Then he made the Pro Bowl in both 2006 and 2007. And then came his big 2008 season. He had at least one sack in 14 of the Cowboys' 16 games.

DeMarcus is not just a great pass rusher, though. He also made 110 tackles in 2008. That was the most of his career. "He's just as good or better against the run," linebacker Zach Thomas says.

That rare combination earned DeMarcus the Butkus Award as the NFL's best linebacker in 2008. Named for Dick Butkus, one of the greatest linebackers in football history, this award has been given to college football's best linebacker. For the first time in 2008, the Butkus Award also was given to the *NFL*'s best linebacker, too. It was an easy choice for the voters.

# JAMES HARRISON
## LB, STEELERS

For as long as the Super Bowl is played, James Harrison's interception return for a touchdown in game XLIII in the 2008 season will make the highlight reels. The Pittsburgh Steelers' linebacker stepped in front of Arizona quarterback Kurt Warner's pass on the last play of the second quarter. Harrison rumbled 100 yards down the right sideline, fending off several attempted tackles. He tumbled across the goal line with no time left in the first half to give Pittsburgh a 17–7 lead. The Steelers went on to win 27–23.

It was the biggest defensive play in the history of the NFL's biggest game. But it also was only one play in a season's worth of game-breaking plays for the fifth-year star. For the year, he had 100 tackles and a club-record 16 sacks. His hard hits forced seven fumbles.

Harrison made so many big plays in 2008, in fact, that the Associated Press named him the NFL's Defensive Player of the Year. That's a big honor for a player who had trouble even making an NFL team out of college. In fact, James was the first undrafted player ever to win the award.

James played college football at Kent State in Kent, Ohio. He was a good player in college — but not a single NFL team thought he was good enough to spend a draft pick on him in 2002. They thought he was too small (although at 6 feet and 242 pounds, he is still a big man) or too slow or didn't play against enough top-notch competition in college.

The Steelers gave him a chance in training camp that year, but they cut him. So did the Baltimore Ravens. Pittsburgh signed him and cut him again two more times. Eventually, James got his chance after injuries to other players. By 2007, he was a Pro Bowl player.

Pittsburgh long has been known for having great defensive players. James Harrison's name is now included among them.

ED REED

# ED REED
## S, RAVENS

**W**ant to find Ed Reed? That's easy. Just look for the football, because the Baltimore Ravens' free safety is usually around it. Football players and coaches call that kind of a player a ball hawk. And there might not be a better ball hawk in the NFL these days than Reed.

Ask Philadelphia Eagles quarterback Kevin Kolb. Midway through the fourth quarter of a game at Baltimore in Week 12 of 2008, the Eagles drove to the Ravens' 1-yard line. On second down, Kolb thought he saw an open receiver in the back of the end zone. He zipped a pass toward his target. But in stepped Reed. Ed intercepted the pass and took off the other way! He didn't stop until he reached Philadelphia's end zone for a back-breaking touchdown. Baltimore went on to win the game 36-7, and Ed's 107-yard touchdown set an NFL record for the longest interception return in history.

Game-breaking plays are nothing new for Ed, though. He's made them routinely ever since the Ravens drafted him out of Miami in the first round in 2002. Guess who held the record for the longest return before his 107-yarder in 2008? That's right, it was Ed. He had a 106-yard interception return for a touchdown against the Cleveland Browns in 2004.

Ed was a full-time starter his first season in the league and a Pro Bowl player in his second. Then, in 2004, he led the NFL when he intercepted nine passes. He returned those thefts for 358 yards, which set another record. He was named the league's Defensive Player of the Year. In 2008, Ed led the league again with nine interceptions. He was the only player in the NFL to be voted a first-team all-pro on every one of the Associated Press ballots.

"The dude is amazing," says Fabian Washington, a cornerback. "He can cover anything on the planet."